LITTLE WOMEN

OPERA IN TWO ACTS

words and music by

MARK ADAMO

after the novel by

Louisa May Alcott

Commissioned by Houston Grand Opera

G. SCHIRMER, *Inc.*

DISTRIBUTED BY

HAL•LEONARD®
CORPORATION

7777 W. BLUEMOUND RD. P.O. BOX 13819 MILWAUKEE, WI 53213

COMPOSER'S NOTE

Little Women, that indispensable chronicle of growing up female in post-Civil War New England, has most often materialized on-screen (and, less successfully, onstage) as the romance of a free-spirited young writer torn between the boy next door and a man of the world. Closer reading of Louisa May Alcott's novel suggested to me a deeper theme: that even those we love will, in all innocence, wound and abandon us until we learn that their destinies are not ours to control. So I shaped a libretto in which Jo's love for her sisters regained the power it wielded in the original novel, and imagined a finale in which Jo at last accepts that even sincerest love and strongest will cannot stave off change and loss.

— MARK ADAMO

CHARACTERS

The March sisters

Jo . . . . mezzo-soprano
Meg . . . . soprano
Beth . . . . soprano
Amy . . . . soprano

Their lovers

Laurie (Theodore Lawrence) . . . . tenor
John Brooke . . . . baritone
Friedrich Bhaer . . . . bass-baritone

Their elders, and others

Alma March . . . . mezzo-soprano
Gideon March / Mr. Dashwood . . . . bass-baritone
Cecilia March . . . . mezzo-soprano/contralto
Quartet of female voices

The action takes place just following the American Civil War.

SYNOPSIS

Prologue

The attic of the March house: slanting light of a dark afternoon.

A shimmer of strings, a tumble of voices ("Four little chests"): Jo, twenty-one but feeling older, sprawled on an ancient sofa, scribbles an elegiac poem until her childhood friend (and would-be lover, once), Laurie, appears in the attic doorway. Delighted, but uneasy—Laurie's just returned from Paris, where he's married Jo's younger sister Amy—Jo presses him: he hasn't married Amy just to remain close to Jo, has he? Worse: in loving Amy ("she's loved beyond compare, loved, loved beyond belief"), Laurie has fallen quite out of love with Jo; can she forgive him? Jo claims relief and good cheer, though a grieving orchestra, oddly, belies her: Laurie, oblivious and exultant, proposes a return to their easy rapport of years ago. Wasn't their relationship "perfect as it was"?

This phrase maddens Jo and deranges the scene: in scathing self-reproach ("Couldn't I un-bake the breads"), Jo mocks the very idea of trying to stop time from changing the ones she loves: and the opera spirals back in time to show us what she means.

Act I

Scene 1. *The attic, two years ago.*

Jo and her three sisters—distracted Meg, ethereal Beth, peppery Amy—bicker and shout as they make a clubhouse of the attic ("Again we meet to celebrate") and games of their household chores. Inducting Laurie as an honorary member of the Barristers' Club, they launch a game of "Truth or Fabrication" while sorting and folding their laundry. The game reveals that Meg's lost glove may actually be part of some deeper secret; that Amy's taunting of Laurie is anything but hostile; that Jo's devotion to her sisters far outweighs her ambitions for her own writing or the very thought of a husband; and that Beth's calm good humor hardens into brittleness at the merest suggestion that her health is unsound. Alma, the girls' mother, summons them to supper. As they go, the close harmony of their last club-song strophe ("Long may our comrades prosper well") seems to affirm their intimacy.

Laurie, lingering, taunts Jo with the knowledge of where Meg's glove is: his tutor, John Brooke, keeps it as a talisman of his love for the older girl, which she may indeed return. Jo, curiously intense, scoffs at the notion that her sister and confidante would "go filling her head with lover-ing rubbish." Laurie, equally intense, reminds her, "Things change," before leaving her alone. Jo, disturbed, starts to rewrite her latest fictional melodrama but can't shake Laurie's hint that Meg might soon leave the family. As she edits "The Curse of the Coventries," Jo argues with an absent Laurie that, Brooke or no Brooke, she and her sisters remain "Perfect as we are."

Scene 2. *The path in front of the March house, weeks later.*

John Brooke walks Meg home in the October twilight. Meg offers to teach him "Rigmarole," a storytelling game, while Jo acts out "The Curse of the Coventries" for an approving Laurie. Brooke's Rigmarole story ("There was a knight, once") is so clearly modeled on his own feelings for Meg that Laurie, overhearing, exults (though he's less amused when Brooke compares him to a colt). An appalled Jo bursts in and all but chases Brooke off, hounding Meg with protests ("He's twenty-eight! He's got one foot in the grave") as they retreat into the house. Inside, an oblivious Beth, at her piano, rewrites her musical setting of verses from *The Pilgrim's Progress* ("She who is down need fear no fall") while Amy sketches a portrait and Alma and her husband Gideon discreetly argue. Jo marshals the entire family to plead with Meg to reject Brooke. Meg, quoting Jo's own "Perfect as we are" music from Scene 1, convinces Jo that rejecting Brooke was her plan all along. No sooner has she given her word than Brooke, arriving unannounced, overwhelms Meg with a bluntly ardent proposal ("Marry me! I love you"). Jo, hidden in the parlor, hisses discouragement; then Cecilia March, the girls' arch and glamorous aunt, sweeps in. Scorning Brooke's profession and suspecting his motives ("He knows you've got wealth in the family"), Cecilia only hardens Meg's resolve: to her own surprise, Meg pledges herself to Brooke. The family congratulates the new couple while Jo, devastated, hears only a haunted memory of the club-song atop an orchestral cortege (Interlude).

Desperate, Jo accuses Meg of abandoning her. Meg, appeasing Jo as best she can, can reply only that "Things change, Jo." But her billowing confession of love for Brooke only wounds Jo more deeply. An implacable Jo withholds forgiveness; Meg, equally implacable, leaves Jo to her anger. Laurie, wordless, tries to console Jo; she, suspicious, shrugs him off. Amy shows Laurie her finished portrait, about which he says exactly the wrong thing. Jo seeks comfort with a sympathetic Beth as October snow begins to fall.

Scene 3. *The March garden, summer of the following year.*

While Alma nervously prepares for Meg's wedding, Amy shows her new sketches to an appreciative Cecilia, and Jo, still resentful, glowers throughout. Meg and Brooke decide to use the same wedding vows that Alma and Gideon had written for their own ceremony years ago. As the parents, assisted by Beth, teach the vows to the young couple ("We stand together"), a feverish Laurie accosts Jo and, to Meg's music of change, confesses his desire for Jo ("It's time things change, Jo, between us"). Jo, to her "Perfect as we are" music, resists; Amy, eavesdropping, overhears their argument as the vows sing on in the distance (Sextet). Finally furious, Jo spurns Laurie; stung and enraged, he flees. Amy, bursting into view, accuses Jo of heartlessness before running off to follow Laurie. Jo, regrouping after the second person in her life has abandoned her for love, strategizes (to the music of her Prologue aria): if she gives Laurie time, and absence, he'll change back from a new and unwelcome lover into the friend she's always cherished. Struck by an idea, she retreats to the house, as Beth, overwhelmed by heat and weakness, collapses at the piano. Meg's cries for help for Beth go unheeded as the act concludes.

Act II

Scene 1. *The publishing offices of* The Daily Volcano, *a fiction tabloid based in New York City, one year later.*

Dashwood, the wry publisher of this New York sensation sheet, grills Jo as to why she's come to town. She tells her story and demands to know if he'll buy "The Curse of the Coventries." Unmoved, he offers her twenty-five dollars for an edited version; Jo, tough as ever, insists on "thirty dollars, and two free copies; I have sisters at home."

Triumphant, Jo returns to her boarding house and writes to her family, which, while loving as ever, is pulling apart under pressure (Letter Scene). Meg and Brooke are struggling with sleeplessness and short temper as the parents of twins; Laurie has abandoned Concord for Oxford; Amy is studying art in Europe under the sponsorship of Cecilia; and Beth's continued denial of her failing health convinces no one but herself. As the scene ends, even Jo finds herself distracted by the offer of an evening at the opera with a new acquaintance at her boarding house, Friedrich Bhaer.

Scene 2. *Jo's boarding house, late that night, after the opera; the March parlor at midnight; a sunny lane on the campus of Oxford, mid-afternoon.*

Jo and Bhaer trade histories and spiritedly argue points of taste while, in Oxford, Amy delicately sounds out Laurie on how much or little he still feels for Jo. Meanwhile, a haunted Beth, doggedly composing at midnight, at last acknowledges the defeat that awaits her and, wordlessly, she rages and mourns in ever-more-dissonant strokes at the piano. Jo, playfully chiding Bhaer for the same aesthetic stiffness she thinks she sees in her father, challenges him to recommend a worthier art than the melodrama she unashamedly enjoys. Bhaer responds by reciting, in the original German, a poem of Goethe's ("Kennst du das land?"). Jo, impressed by his grandeur but not his unintelligibility, requests a translation. Bhaer's English rendering ("Do you know the land?") is, as Brooke's "Rigmarole" was, a confession of love under a mask of storytelling. Jo, moved despite herself, is distracted by a desperate telegram from Alma: Beth has taken a turn for the worse. Rejecting Friedrich's support, Jo flees back to Concord.

Scene 3. *Beth's bedroom, three sleepless nights later.*

A translucent Beth dozes in a throne of pillows as her family keeps vigil. A disheveled Jo bursts in; Beth bids her family leave the two of them alone. Frantic, Jo plumps pillows and prattles about a possible restorative trip to the seaside before Beth, with a hint of her old force, silences her. She urges Jo to accept her impending death

("Have peace, Jo"), which Jo resists until she recognizes, in Beth's music, the same leitmotif of change that formed Meg's and Laurie's utterances of a year ago. "Mother and father: you're all they've got now. Promise me you'll take care of them," Beth insists. Jo accedes. Relieved, spent, Beth drowses, and Jo drowses beside her. When Jo awakes, Beth has died. The orchestra finishes the chorale Beth did not complete as Jo remembers the vanished harmony of her sisters' voices.

Scene 4. *The path in front of the March house, the following spring.*

Jo, a wraith in a dark dress, sweeps the front steps while Cecilia baits her with Amy's latest letter, which relates that she is now, at last, "loved beyond compare, loved, loved beyond belief" by Laurie. A weary Jo accepts the news, and, pressed by Cecilia, admits that Friedrich Bhaer seems to have abandoned her as well: no letters from him have arrived. Strangely satisfied, Cecilia announces to Jo that she's revised her will to leave Plumfield, her orchard estate, to Jo: her death will render Jo independent for the rest of her life. Stunned, if grateful, Jo asks why; and Cecilia, in seductive minuet, urges Jo to use her pending wealth and power, as she, Cecilia, has done, to isolate herself from the pain that loving others (like Meg, Laurie, Beth) is bound to inflict ("You, alone"). Jo recognizes Cecilia's music as a nightmare transformation of her own "Perfect as we are" theme: appalled at this aural vision of her possible future, she rejects the stunned Cecilia and flees to the attic.

Scene 5. *The attic.*

"What endures?" Jo asks no one, flinging herself on the sofa: and the same shimmer of strings and tumble of voices ("Four little chests") brings us back to the very moments in which the opera began. Laurie, as before, enters the attic, apologizing to Jo and suggesting, innocently, that they two go back to the "perfect way it was"; but this time Jo demurs. "The happy old times can't come back, and we mustn't expect it," she tells him. Relieved, admiring, Laurie leaves her in peace. Overwhelmed by feeling, Jo calls on her memories of the sisters of her girlhood ("Barristers! It's quarter past") and, ghostlike, they materialize. In forgiveness and gratitude, she celebrates what they were and releases them to what they are now ("Let me look at you"): they join in harmony a final time before disappearing forever.

Unexpectedly, the attic door opens a third time: it's not Laurie, but Friedrich, in town by chance and eager to see her. "Is now the good moment?" he asks. "Now is all there is," Jo realizes: she extends her hand to him as the opera concludes.

LITTLE WOMEN

PROLOGUE

(Concord, Massachusetts. The 1870s. The attic of the March house: dusty, not uncluttered, but a living space, a refuge. Slanting light of a dark afternoon. Upstage, glimpsed as if through mist, four chests, each with a name—Meg, Jo, Beth, Amy—carved into the lid.)

QUARTET OF FEMALE VOICES
(ghostly)

Four little chests all in a row,
Dim with dust, and worn by time,
All fashioned and filled, long ago,
By children now in their prime.
Four little names, one on each lid,
Carved out by a boyish hand,
And underneath, there lieth hid...

(Light finds Jo, 21 but feeling older, collapsed on a sofa in a dark dress. Only a woman of tremendous energy could look this depressed. Her open notebook lies tossed nearby. She retrieves it, resumes writing.)

JO & QUARTET

Histories of the happy band,

JO

The happy, happy band...

(A shaft of light shoots up from the floor; Laurie—21, vital, handsome, nervous today—has opened the attic door.)

JO
(delighted)

Laurie!

LAURIE
(*mock-courtly*)

The very same, madam.

Jo

Christopher Columbus!

JO & LAURIE

Hello...

LAURIE

Another potboiler?

Jo
(*closing her book*)

Not this time.
Sentimental rubbish; won't earn a dime.
Christopher Columbus, look at you.

LAURIE

I've hardly changed.

Jo

Small ways.
(*circling him*)
Bigger. Bonnier. Otherwise,
The same scapegrace as always.

LAURIE

It's wonderful to see you, Jo…

JO & LAURIE
(*awkwardly*)

So...

Jo
(*brightly*)

Actually married!
(*laughing*)
I'm vexed.
What horrible thing will you do next?

LAURIE

I did it to please your sister.

Jo

Fib! She did it to please you,
I'd swear.
Again, sir, the truth! If you dare.
(*They're still joking, but Jo has a bit of an edge.*)

LAURIE
(*evasively*)
Well, we'd planned to come home with the Carrolls,
A month or more ago...

Jo

That's not what I mean, Laurie—

LAURIE

But Mrs. Carroll rather fancies Paris in the snow...

Jo

Laurie!

LAURIE

Then Grandpa wanted to come home, but I couldn't let him go, so—

Jo

Laurie!
(*cryptically*)
Mozart!

LAURIE

What?

Jo

"He couldn't have one sister,
So he took the other, and was happy."
You told me that story yourself.

LAURIE

Jo!

JO
(*indignant*)

I have to know, Laurie,
I have to know!
Amy deserves, Amy deserves to be loved.
Tell me, Laurie.

LAURIE
(*simply*)

She's loved.
She's loved.
Loved beyond compare,
Loved, loved beyond belief.

JO

Oh!
(*floored, devastated, but putting on her best face*)
Well.
That's a relief.

LAURIE
(*apologetic*)

She really is best for me.
You knew it before I did.

JO
(*blustering*)

Well, *we* quarreled like magpies.

LAURIE

I shall never stop loving you, Jo—

JO
(*forgiving*)

I know.

LAURIE

It's just—

JO

Altered.

LAURIE

Exactly.

JO

We were meant to be friends.

LAURIE

You knew it; you tried to tell me—

JO

I wasn't so smart.

LAURIE

And then, later, I was—

JO & LAURIE

So confused,

LAURIE

And then Amy, in England—

JO

We changed places in your heart.

LAURIE

Jo—can you forgive me?

JO
(laughing)

Laurie.
Forgive you?
There's nothing to forgive.
Love her,
Love her, long as you both shall live.
I wish you every joy.
Just tell me one thing.

LAURIE

Ask it.

JO

Who obeys?
Amy or my boy?

LAURIE
(*mistaking her attempt at humor for the real thing*)
Now you're beginning to marm it!

JO
Mmm…

LAURIE
I'd hoped I could count on you—
I should have known I could!

JO
(*absently*)
Rock of Gibraltar.

LAURIE
Ah, Jo!
So we can be just best friends again—

JO
Well—

LAURIE
Best friends for good?

JO
(*cautiously*)
You know I'll always be your friend, Laurie…

LAURIE
You know, Jo, it was truly perfect—perfect—
Perfect as it was.
Perfect as it wa—

JO
(*beyond incredulous*)
What did you say?

LAURIE
(*innocent*)
Wasn't it perfect as it was?

(Jo laughs, at first weakly, then with increasing mania.)

LAURIE

What did I say?

JO

Perfect as it was! Perfect as it was!
Oh, yes indeed!

LAURIE
(a bit terrified)

Jo? Jo!

JO
(fiercely)

Let's just—go back to the way it was?
Just like that!
Back to the perfect way it was.

LAURIE

I didn't mean—

JO

Why not?
And perhaps I know how.
(The light shifts. We have left reality; we are in Jo's fantasy. Laurie stands frozen. Jo waves her hand at him, as if she were a sorceress. Laurie starts to sing his last speech backwards, and moves, marionette-like, in reverse.)

LAURIE

Was it as perfect. Jo, know you good for friends best again friends
Just be can we so Jo! Ah, could I known have
Should I you on count could I hoped I'd…
(He vanishes down the stairs, the way he came.)

JO
(self-satisfied, addressing audience)

That worked for the moment.
But, with so many, so many capital reasons
To cross out the calendar, roll back the seasons,
Why stop with now?
(with furious glee)

Couldn't I
Un-bake the breads,
Unweave the mittens,
Un-feed the cats, see 'em
Shrink back to kittens?
Just give me a moment... to
Unmake the beds,
Un-brew the tea,
Paste every fallen leaf back on the tree.
I'll just need a moment…
Why fancy time an immovable line?
Why not as a ball of magical twine?
Rewind the spool—
Aha, ha-ha! April Fool!
No one's fighting, nor flirting,
Not deceiving, denying;
No one's hurting,
No one's leaving,
No one's dying,
Everything's fine!
Everything's fine!
So just watch me un-trim the boughs,
Un-slice the pies,
Blow every snowfall back up to the skies.
I'll just need a moment,
And all of us can unsay the vows,
Un-cry the tears,
Un-ring the wedding chimes,
Bring back the happy times,
Only give me a moment—
No—no—no!
I want *all* of our moments,
All of our years!
(*Jo shakes her hair down around her shoulders; we burst into Act I.*)

ACT I

Scene One

(The attic. Late on a Saturday afternoon, late summer, 3 years ago. Jo barrels into the room as an elegant Meg of 19, an ethereal Beth of 17, a peppery Amy of 15, and a Laurie of 18 assemble, hauling three laundry bags. Each takes from her trunk—or his pocket—a badge and a lensless spectacle. Jo, who dons a false moustache, helps Meg unspool a homemade-looking banner lettered THE COURT OF LAST RESORT. The mood is festive, but ordinary; this is a game they look forward to each week, but it's still a week like any other.)

JO

Barristers! It's quarter past! No time to waste!

AMY, BETH, MEG

Settle your wig, Jo.

AMY
(complaining)

Why "barristers"? Why not "ladies of the law"?

JO

Beth! No!

(Beth is moving her trunk.)

BETH

I'm perfectly fine.

JO

Sit.

LAURIE

Jo would know best.

JO

You'll never get well if you don't rest!

LAURIE

What's wrong with "barristers," Amy?

AMY

Ugh!

BETH
(gently, firmly)

I am well, Jo, I am.

MEG
(serious)

Jo is right, it isn't best for you, lamb.

AMY

It just seems horridly masculine, is all.

MEG
(intently)

Do you know that I have still not found my glove?
The ivory one?
I thought I'd left the pair of them over at Laurie's,
But Mr. Brooke only found one.

JO

I bought you a new pair.

LAURIE
(slyly)

My tutor, Brooke?

MEG
(to Laurie)

Of course! What other Mr. Brooke is there?

LAURIE

You tell me.

JO

Barristers! Stations?

AMY, BETH, MEG, LAURIE
(wearily)

Aye.

JO

Badges?

AMY, BETH, MEG, LAURIE

Aye.

JO

Spectacles?

AMY, BETH, MEG, LAURIE

Aye.

JO

Maestra Elizabeth,
The opening anthem, if you please.

(*Beth hums a pitch.*)

AMY, BETH, MEG, JO

Again we meet to celebrate
With badge and solemn rite
Our fifty-second anniversary—

AMY

Fifty-first—Meg's cold—

JO
(*dryly*)

Thanks.

AMY, BETH, MEG, JO

Our fifty-*first* anniversary
In Barrister Hall tonight.
We all are here in perfect health,
None gone from our small band;
Again we see each well-known face
And press each friendly hand.
Long may our comrades prosper well,
Our club unbroken be,
And coming years their blessings pour
On our sorority.

(Meg, singing the third of the chord, sags in pitch. Beth gestures frantically, and she corrects it.)

MEG
(airily)

Major, minor…

JO

First, everyone, welcome our neighbor and newest member—

AMY
(coolly)

Honorary.

MEG

Behave.

JO
(overriding)

The estimable Theodore Lawrence, known as Laurie—

LAURIE
(very courtly)

Who devotes himself to the Barristers Club
Nigh unto the grave.

BETH
(seduced)

Thank you.

MEG

Show-off.

JO

Now—
(Jo gestures, and Beth presents a laundry bag.)

LAURIE

Wait—
Mr. Chairman, I forget the rules.

MEG

It's very easy. We call it—

AMY, BETH, MEG, JO

Truth or Fabrication!

MEG

We've sorted the laundry by type;
Sheets, stockings, whatnot—

AMY

But nothing too private for you to see.

MEG

The person who folds the last piece
Must answer three questions.

JO

Truthfully!
Think you can do it, Laurie?

LAURIE

Nothing to it.

JO

Fair enough. Ready?

AMY & LAURIE

Ready.
(*Amy exchanges glances with Laurie.*)

MEG

Ready.

BETH

Ready.

(*Jo dumps out the contents of Beth's bag.*)

JO

Socks!

(*They dig into Beth's bag, folding madly and chattering the while.*)

BETH

Needs a patch.

AMY

What is this shade?

MEG

This sort-of rose?

BETH

So awfully worn...

JO

Well, these don't match.

BETH

And utterly frayed.

AMY

You're stretching those.

MEG

My heel is torn!

AMY

It's more a fuchsia.

JO

It's only color!

BETH

And still not clean—confound this grease!

JO

Oh, fashion minutia: is anything duller?

AMY & MEG

Something between maroon and cerise—

JO

Aha!

(All eyes on Meg, who deliberately takes the last pair of socks out of the bag, holds it upside-down to prove it's empty, and folds the socks.)

JO
(*chanting*)

Truth... truth... truth... truth...

AMY, BETH, JO, LAURIE

Truth... truth... truth... truth...
Truth... truth... truth... truth...

MEG

Very well.
Three questions, no more.
I'm prepared.

(*The others continue chanting in the background.*)

AMY

Who's your best friend?

MEG

Jo.

JO

Who are your heroines?

MEG

Marmee, and Jenny Lind.

LAURIE
(*slyly*)

Don't you really know where your glove is?

MEG

No.

(*General laughing protest... except from Jo.*)

AMY

Not so likely!

BETH

Meg, really—

LAURIE

Indeed!

MEG

You didn't ask me my *suspicions*.
Truth is a hard game, Laurie.

LAURIE

Touché.

JO

All right... ready?

AMY & LAURIE
(intentionally simultaneous this time)

Ready.

MEG

Ready.

BETH

Ready.

JO

Linens!

BETH

Beautiful violet!

AMY

Needs a pressing...

MEG

There's a name for these kinds of laces...

AMY

Isn't it "eyelet"? Only guessing...

JO

These are those same pillowcases?

MEG

Fading, slightly...

AMY

This didn't shrink!

BETH

A touch of bleach, there...

JO

I've forgotten.

BETH

White with white,

AMY & BETH

Pink with pink,

AMY, BETH, MEG

And peach with peach.

JO

It wasn't cotton.

LAURIE

Aha!

(Jo's the victim this time.)

AMY, BETH, MEG, LAURIE

Truth... truth... truth... truth...
Truth... truth... truth... truth...

JO

Do your worst.

AMY

What's your greatest virtue?

JO

Persistence.

LAURIE

Where do you most want to live?

JO

Wherever my sisters are.

MEG

What do you most value in a husband?

JO

Nonexistence.

AMY

Tell the truth, Jo!

LAURIE

That's encouraging, I must say.

JO

I am!

MEG

Jo's perverse. Now, everyone:
Ready?

LAURIE & AMY

Ready.

BETH

Ready.

JO

Ready.

(Meg pulls out the first of the…)

MEG

Work clothes!

(They dig into Meg's bag this time.)

AMY

Favorite smock…

MEG

The polka dots?

JO
(scoffing)

Polka dots!

BETH

Peculiar plaid.

MEG

Re-hem the skirt...

JO

A laughingstock!

MEG

And tied in knots…

BETH

I ripped it badly.

AMY

Father's shirt...

MEG

And Mother's bonnet…

AMY

Horrid stain!

MEG

It looks like eggs.

BETH

The stitching shows.

JO

I spilt tea on it.

BETH

It's not so plain...

AMY

Now, is this Meg's, or is this J—
Oh, no.
(It's her turn.)
I loathe this game, and I always have.

BETH, MEG, JO, LAURIE

Truth... truth... truth... truth...

JO

What's the trial of your life?

AMY

The way my nose is made.

LAURIE

What's your greatest ambition?

AMY

To paint like Raphael.

MEG

What's your greatest strength?

AMY
(directly to Laurie)

My power to persuade.

JO

That's for certain.
Strong men, fear!

AMY
(testily)

Meaning?

MEG

Amy—

BETH

Barristers.
(She stands there, radiating authority.)

                              LAURIE
I'd almost forgotten you were here.

                              BETH
Ready?

                              LAURIE
Ready.

                              AMY
                    (intentionally out of sync)
Ready.

                              JO
Ready.

                              MEG
Ready.

                              BETH
Um... we're out of laundry.

(Playfully intimidating, they crowd around Beth.)

                              MEG
I guess you're volunteering.

                              AMY
We're already through.

                              LAURIE
And I'm too new.

                    AMY, MEG, JO, LAURIE
Truth... truth... truth!

                              BETH
All right!
So domineering.

                              JO
What do you most wish for?

BETH

The music to that Schumann song.

AMY

What's your greatest fault?

BETH

Being afraid of people.

LAURIE

What do you want to be in twenty years?
(*An awkward moment; he continues, oblivious.*)
Or ten years?

JO
(*warning*)

Laurie—

BETH
(*unblinking*)

Strong.

ALMA
(*from offstage*)

Girls!

JO

Laurie—we'll talk later.

ALMA
(*poking her head up the attic stairs*)

Supper, half an hour!
Volunteers?
Anyone who's able.

BETH, MEG, JO

We'll be right down, Mother.

AMY
(*attempting slyness*)

I'd love to help, Marmee,
But the soup might stain,
And my dress is white.

ALMA

Terribly thoughtful of you, dear.
You can lay the table.

JO

Nice try.
Everyone! Closing verse.
(She hums a pitch. All sisters hurriedly join hands.)

AMY, BETH, MEG, JO

Long may our comrades prosper well,
Our club unbroken be;
And coming years their blessings pour
On our sorority.
(In this moment we see how loving this circle of women is. But Meg, to Beth's despair, still goes flat on the last pitch.)

BETH
(affectionately)

Sopranos.

JO

Everyone, give me your badges:
I'll put up here, and I'll be there.

LAURIE

I'll help too, Madam Mother.

ALMA

Thank you, Laurie.
You'll stay for supper, I hope:
Only chowder, but you're welcome to share.

JO

Of course he'll stay—won't you, Laurie?

ALMA

Quarter hour, downstairs.

MEG

Marmee, I meant to ask—
My glove—the ivory one?

(All but Jo and Laurie have vanished downstairs.)

JO

You got off easy.
We'll get to you next.

LAURIE

Do you want to know a secret?

JO

What?

LAURIE

Keep it under your hat.

JO

Fine.

LAURIE

Ready?

JO

Yes.

LAURIE

Really?

JO

Laurie—

LAURIE
(grandly)

I know where Meg's glove is.

JO

I should be thrilled about that?

LAURIE

Wait till I tell you.

JO

Tell me.

(Laurie whispers in Jo's ear. Jo is appalled.)

JO

How do you know?

LAURIE

Saw it.

JO

Where?

LAURIE

Lesson, Saturday morning.

JO

Ugh!
All this time?

LAURIE

Yes.
Ain't it romantic?

JO

No, it's horrid—it cannot be borne.

LAURIE

I'd hoped you'd be pleased.

JO

Pleased? At anyone taking Meg away?

LAURIE

You'll feel better about it
When someone comes to take you away.

JO

Me? Ha! Don't be alarmed.
Nobody'll want me.

LAURIE
(seriously)

You won't give anyone the time of day.

(This is a conversation Laurie keeps trying to have. Jo will have none of it.)

JO

I don't like that sort of thing.
I think it's horrible to break up families so.

LAURIE

Some might say the families grow.

JO

Besides, Brooke is Brooke,
But I know my Meg—

LAURIE

Do you?

JO

She's far too sensible to go
Filling her head with lover-ing rubbish!
The very idea's deranged.

LAURIE

You never know, Jo—
Things change.
I'll see you down below.
(He leaves her in the garret. She is still—then picks up her notebook and pen.)

JO
(reviewing her draft, rapidly)
"The Curse of the Coventries:
A Thrilling Romance." Draft Two.
Gondola after gondola, yes,
Brilliant throng, marble staircase, but wait!
Masked avenger,
"Not my child!" cried she,
The count, in a perfect… perfect…
Madness?—no. Mania?—no.
The count, in a perfect... perfect...
(The word eludes her. Laurie has distracted her too much. He's gone, but she addresses him anyway.)
Look at us, Laurie:
We're perfect as we are—

Perfect as we are, truly perfect as we are.
See how we adore each other?
See the way we blend?
How often are your sisters, your nearest sisters,
Your dearest friends?
Your dearest friends... zy.
(*Having put her anxiety to rest, the word comes to her.*)
Frenzy. Yes!
The count, in a perfect frenzy, delivered a
Stunning—ouch!—blow to the head!
The villain, cackling,
(*she cackles*)
Nya, nya, nya,
Robed in red,
Raised his pike for another strike—
(*screaming*)
Ah!
But our hero, happily, helmeted,
Got him a grip on the villain's throat—
"Die, ye varlet, die!"
And squeezed,
And squeezed,
And shook him until his eyeballs bled—
Then kicked him out of the chamber, down the
Corridor, out of the window and into the moat.
When suddenly a
Spectral?—no. Ghostly?—dull.
Suddenly a... a... a...
(*The memory of Laurie's words has derailed her imagination again.*)
Ah, admit it, Laurie—
Are we not perfect as we are?
Perfect as we are, absolutely perfect as we are.
You've known us now for years and years.
I ask you, as a brother,
What's out there that the world can give we don't already
Give each other?
What don't we give each other... worldly.
Otherworldly. Yes!
An otherworldly figure,
All in white, whispered:

"Here! Here!
Here is the prize you seek."
They paused before an oaken door
Which swung forth with a creak.
Yes—rejoice! He knew that voice!
His luckless lady's cries!
"Save me! Save me!"
He sprang forth to collect her—
"Here, my lady, here!"
But—"No! No!" groaned the spectre,
And waved before his eyes the... the...
And waved before his eyes the...
Dazzling?—no. Glittering?—hmm...
Gorgeous?—too ripe. Pricey?—too coarse.
Of course, there are tears.
Of course, there are quarrels.
Today, it's smiles,
Tomorrow, snarls.
There are days on end we drift apart,
Each of us doing, perfecting, pursuing her art...

(We see, for a moment, in other parts of the house, Amy sketching Alma, and Beth coaching Meg at the piano.)

But comes the day
We hate the song,
The sketch is wrong,
The story's long—
Then comes the day...
We come together again!
We come together again!
Turn to each other to revive us,
Refresh us.
Is "lovering," is anything more precious?
"And waved before him the...
Precious, Coventry Emerald!"
(She closes the notebook.)
Well, that's a potboiler.
No, my clever Laurie—
We're perfect as we are.

Perfect as we are, ever perfect as we are.
Let the days go by,
Let the seasons fly,
Let the moonstruck Romeos
Crowd 'round my sisters' door.
They don't know what my sisters know:
It's families, it's families that endure.
(*She looks at her sisters again, as they fade from view.*)
How grateful I am...
(*laughing*)
Brooke!

Scene Two

(*The path in front of the March house, weeks later. Twilight. Meg and Brooke—quiet, keen-eyed, maybe 30—walking. Courtly, but low-key.*)

BROOKE

"Rigmarole"?

MEG

It's another game. The word is Italian.
I'd teach you Truth or Fabrication;
But we're missing some crucial props.

(*Jo and Laurie appear.*)

JO
(dramatizing)

"Die, ye varlet, die!"
And squeezed,
And squeezed,
And shook him until his eyeballs bled—

LAURIE

Ho!

JO

I know—blood. You've *got* to have blood.
—Then kicked him out of the chamber,
Down the corridor, out of the window
And into the moat.

(They disappear.)

                                   MEG
You start to tell a story,
Anything you like, for as long as you like—
But you stop at the most exciting part...

(Jo and Laurie reappear, walking and out of breath.)

                                  LAURIE
No, it's capital.
Better than that rubbish in
The Blarneystone Banner.
The atmosphere!

                                    JO
And more salable than Pa's essays.
If only I could take myself to the city!
But my sisters need me here.

                                  LAURIE
                                (pointing)
Look!

                                    JO
What?

                                  LAURIE
I told you.

                                   MEG
...When the next one takes it up and does the same.
Would you like me to start?

                                  LAURIE
Poetry in motion!

                                    JO
Shh!

BROOKE

Actually, I already have a notion.
There was a knight, once—
No crusader, no hero, no one great;
But not a dunce, either—

MEG

How old was he?

BROOKE

Twenty-eight.

(Meg registers the similarity between the teller and the tale.)

LAURIE

Sly!

JO

Why?

LAURIE

He's twenty-eight.

JO
(outraged)

That's unfair play.

BROOKE

He met a duke, one day,
Who'd bred a colt—fine and strong, but young and wild.
Said the duke: "Train him—
But train him tenderly, as you would train a child."

LAURIE

Oh, Brooke, you'll suffer tomorrow.

JO

I cannot hear him!

LAURIE

He's calling me an animal!

Jo

Shh!

Brooke

"I shall try," said the knight.
"One can only try.
I'll be kind when I can;
I'll be patient when I must.
Still, each day, bright or gray, I'll be nigh.
Shall I try?" asked the knight...

Meg

Then what happened?

Brooke

They got on slowly but surely,
And soon the colt grew tame and fond.
(*He looks at Meg. She looks away.*)

Laurie

He flatters himself.

Brooke

Shall I go on?

Jo
(horrified)

She's falling for it!

Meg

Please.

Brooke

One day in town, riding
Past the window of a house he'd never seen,
He spied a maid, reading—

Meg

How old was she?

Brooke

Just nineteen.

JO

He's a weasel.

BROOKE

She seemed serene, noble,
The kind of maid to whom a knight could pledge his life.
But he was poor, and simple—
What could he do to make her want to be his wife?

JO

Fall on your sword?

LAURIE

Jo!

JO
(logically)

He pledged his life.

BROOKE

"I can try," thought the knight.
"One can always try.
I'll pray and I'll plan,
Be as patient as I must—
I'll do all that I can
To be worthy of her trust,
And each day, bright or gray, I'll be nigh.
Shall I try?" thought the knight.
"Shall I try?" thought the knight.
Miss March,
Miss March,
Miss March,
Shall I try?
(He produces her glove—the ivory one—and presses it into her hand.)

JO

Oh, this cannot be borne.

MEG
(wavering)

Mr. Brooke—

(Jo bursts into Meg's view, Laurie in tow.)

JO

When suddenly the heavens opened, thunder rolled, and
The knight was struck—bam!—by a bolt of lightning,
And was shriveled to a crisp.
Pity. Well...
(threatening)
These things happen.

MEG
(dryly)

You know my sister.

BROOKE

Indeed.

LAURIE

Brooke! Good to
(whinnying)
See-ee-ee-ee you.
(He stamps his foot on the ground and flashes Brooke a grin a mile wide.)

JO

Awfully late, Meg, don't you think?

MEG

Please forgive us, Mr. Brooke—
We likely should be going.

BROOKE

I understand completely.

LAURIE

Us, too, Brooke, time to go
(whinnying)
I-i-i-i-in.
'Night, Meg.

MEG

'Night, Laurie.

                              LAURIE

'Night, Jo.

                               JO

'Night, Laurie.

                             BROOKE

Margaret?

                              MEG

Yes?

                             BROOKE
                            (gently)

If it's all right with you—
I'd like to speak to your father.

                              MEG
                      (inwardly thrilled)

He's home this evening... John.

                          BROOKE & MEG

Good night.
Good night.

                               JO
                   (all but chasing him off)

Good night, good night, good night!

                              LAURIE
                           (brightly)

Hey!
Got any sugar?
(whickers slyly)
Want a ride?

(Brooke and Laurie set off.)

                               JO

"John"? "John"?

MEG

I don't wish to speak to you right now.

JO
(stalking Meg up the path and into the house)
"I'll be home, *John*."
"I'll just be embroidering your name on a sampler, *John*."

MEG

You're depraved.

JO

He's twenty-eight!
He's got one foot in the grave!

(They have by this time entered the March parlor and its adjoining hall. Gideon March—40, priestly but with a glint—beside Beth, at the piano. Alma, writing checks, and Amy sketching nearby.)

BETH

"She that is down need fear no fall,
She that is low..."
Hmmm...

ALMA

Father, if you let them reprint *Inscriptions*,
We could just pay the butcher.

BETH
(rewriting)
"She *who* is low, no pride."

MEG
(offstage, exasperated)
Honestly!

ALMA

Gideon?

GIDEON

The Niles publish entertainment.
They do not publish thought.

BETH

"She who is humble ever shall…"

MEG
(*entering*)

Hello, Father. Hello, Beth.
Jo's plaguing my life out.

JO
(*pursuing*)

Fib!

ALMA

There's nothing immoral in recompense.

BETH

"Have God to be her guide."

JO
(*mocking*)

Your John.

MEG

Don't say "my John," it isn't proper or true.

GIDEON

What price integrity, Alma?

JO
(*edgily*)

Dear Pa!

ALMA

This month, eighteen dollars…

GIDEON
(*dismissive*)

Bah!

ALMA

And seventy-one cents.

BETH

"I am content with what I have."

AMY

Incidentally, everyone,
Aunt is due any moment.
(*avidly*)
Laurie!

BETH
(*dissatisfied*)

"Little—" The vowel!
(*She drops her hand on the keyboard.*)

LAURIE
(*entering*)

Hello.
(*commenting on the "chord" Beth just sounded*)
Modern.

AMY

She's working, as am I!
(*She displays her sketchpad.*)

GIDEON

Wonderful news about Oxford, Lawrence.

LAURIE

Thanks. Still a year away!

ALMA
(*wearily*)
Well, what's another month's credit between friends?

BETH

"Naught be it or much—"
We need the third.

JO
(*tormenting Meg*)

"John… John… John…"

MEG

You're relentless.

BETH

"Naught be it or much."

GIDEON

I'd like to hear this hymn, please, if all agree.

BETH

"And, Lord, contentment still I crave,
Because…"
(noticing the silence)
What?

ALMA

Nothing, dear, we're just listening.

BETH
(defensively)

Oh. Well. It's not done.

AMY, MEG, JO, ALMA, LAURIE, GIDEON
(patiently)

We know.

BETH

"Fulness to them a burden is
Who go on Pilgrimage;
Here, little, and hereafter, bliss,
Is best from age to age."
I don't like the ending yet; but something like that.

AMY

Our own Fanny Mendelssohn!

JO
(outraged)

Christopher Columbus, "tame and fond"!
You're considering a man who compares
Courting a woman to breaking a horse!

MEG
(coolly)

I won't consider anything until he speaks,
And he won't,
Because father said I was too young.

GIDEON

Meg and your mother and I have discussed this at length.

JO
(pleading for allies)

Look at her, Father!
If he did speak, she wouldn't know what to say.

MEG

Truly?

JO

Yes, truly.
You'd cry, or blush, or let him have his own way,
Instead of giving him a good, decided "No."

ALMA

You underestimate your sister's strength.

MEG
(boasting)

In fact, I know just what I should say.
I've prepared.

JO
(a dare)

Tell.

AMY

Make it elegant.

MEG
(directly to Jo)

"Thank you, Mr. Brooke,
You're very kind, but I am too young to consider;
So let us say no more.
Let us but continue as before."

(She's quoting Jo's theme from Scene One. Jo's touched.)

JO & MEG

See how we adore each other?
See the way we blend?
How often are your sisters,
Your nearest sisters,
Your dearest friends?
Your dearest friends?

(There is a knock at the door.)

LAURIE

He wastes no time.

JO

Circling for the kill!

AMY, BETH, ALMA, GIDEON

Jo!

MEG

You're just impossible.
It's probably Aunt.
(She leaves the room to answer the door. Jo, trailing, slides behind the drapes.)

JO
(innocently)

Don't mind me.

(Meg opens the door. Brooke, all composure gone, grabs for Meg's hand.)

BROOKE

Marry me!
I love you.

(Meg, totally nonplussed, deserts him on the step, and turns to Jo.)

MEG
(disarmed)

He loves—

JO
(hissing)

I love you, Mother loves you, everyone loves you,
That's not the point!

MEG
(rapt)

Love—

JO
(commanding)

"Thank you, Mr. Brooke, you're very kind,
BUT!"

(Meg hurries back to Brooke.)

MEG
(reciting)

Thank you, Mr. Brooke—

BROOKE

John.

MEG

John...

(Behind the drapes, Jo screams in frustration.)

MEG

I don't know.

BROOKE

If you could find out?
(politely)
Your curtains are writhing.

MEG

It's an old house.
(desperately)
I'm too young.

BROOKE

I'll wait. Meanwhile, you could be learning to like me.
Would it be a hard lesson, dear?

MEG

Not if I choose to learn it, but—

BROOKE
(a bit glib)

Please choose, Meg. I love to teach,
And this is easier than training a colt.

(Jo whinnies harshly. Meg deserts Brooke again.)

JO

What color saddle, Mrs. Brooke?
Chestnut would bring out your eyes.

(This gets Meg. She wheels back to Brooke.)

MEG

I don't choose.
Go away, and leave me be!

BROOKE
(stunned)

Truly?

MEG
(stonily)

Yes.

BROOKE

I mayn't change your mind?
Let me try, Meg.
Let me only try!
Let me pray, let me plan.
Be as patient as I must.
I'll do all that I can
To be worthy of your trust,
And each day, bright or gray, I'll be nigh...

CECILIA
(entering, grandly)

Young man,
Trust me,
Never, ever beg.

MEG

Aunt March!

CECILIA

Margaret.

MEG

Mr. John Brooke, Laurie's tutor.
Joh—Mr. Brooke, Miss Cecilia March.

CECILIA

You're red as a peony.

MEG
(hinting)

Mr. Brooke came to see Father.

BROOKE
(timidly)

Honored to meet you.

CECILIA
(gaily)

How right you are.

(Brooke, heeding Meg, retreats to the parlor, and pleads his case to Gideon and Alma.
Amy, avid, watches Laurie, who, with Beth, eavesdrops on the hall.)

MEG
(breezily)

So, how goes it at Plumfield?

CECILIA
(no-nonsense)

Don't dissemble, dear.
Jo's told me her suspicions.
You haven't accepted him, have you?

MEG

Hush! He'll hear!

CECILIA

Disaster.
This tutor—
Has he a business?

MEG

Teaching *is* his business.

CECILIA

Wealth in the family?

MEG

He has many warm friends.

CECILIA
(*as if to a child*)

Meg,
Friends are not wealth.
Wealth is wealth. Meg. Meg!
(*impatient*)
Your family needs you to make a rich match!

MEG
(*a bit riled*)

John is sure to get on;
He's smart and brave, got heaps of talent—
I'm proud to think he cares for me.

CECILIA
(*airily*)

You miss the obvious.
He knows you've got wealth in the family.

MEG

Aunt March, how dare you?

(*In the parlor, Brooke and the family, the matter settled, are now listening in.*)

My John wouldn't marry for money
Any more than I would.
I'm not afraid of being poor—
And he loves me.

CECILIA
(*patiently*)

Margaret. That's your parents talking,
And they are babies.
You don't marry a man because you love him.

MEG

I do.

CECILIA

Do you hear this?
Accept him, and not one penny,
Not one penny of my money goes to you.

MEG

I shall marry whom I please, Aunt March.
Leave your money to whomever you'd like.

CECILIA

You disappoint me.
(*stroking Meg's cheek*)
This face! and you toss it away.
Well. I'd planned to see my brother,
But I've had quite enough already of the company of fools.
(*sweetly*)
Jo, dear! Unless you've succeeded by now in
Hanging yourself by the curtain pull,
Tell Gideon to expect a letter.
(*to Meg, coldly*)
You've lost more than you know.
(*She withdraws. Jo, devastated, eyes Meg.*)

JO

What have you done?

(*Then Brooke bursts into view.*)

MEG

I didn't know how much I cared, till she maligned you.
(*She folds herself into his arms.*)

BROOKE

Sister Jo, congratulate us!

(*Jo, mute, curtseys elaborately and, like a court jester, leads them back into the parlor, where, in eerily slow pantomime, the family makes much of the new couple. Jo cleaves to the wall; her silence is lost on neither Laurie nor Beth.*)

QUARTET OF FEMALE VOICES

Long may our comrades prosper well,
Our club unbroken, unbroken, unbroken be...
Unbroken... unbroken...

(*Returning to normal movement, Meg leads Brooke to the hall, passing Jo on the way out. No shyness now; they're a couple. The parlor darkens.*)

BROOKE

Don't it seem very long to wait?

MEG

So much to learn before I shall be ready!

BROOKE & MEG

So we'll work and we'll plan,
Be as patient as we must,
Till that day, our day, draws nigh.

BROOKE

Sister Jo...

(*Jo is not forthcoming. Surrendering, Brooke embraces Meg and leaves. Jo and Meg are alone. Jo whinnies again, harshly.*)

MEG

Don't be so literal.
I'll be training him, too.

JO

He'll never let you sing, you know.

MEG

He loves my voice, actually.

JO

I should marry you myself,
And keep you safe in the family.

MEG

Well, you can't.
And I wouldn't marry you if you could.

JO

Meg!

MEG

You're the wrong height.

JO

Why don't you love me anymore?

MEG

I love you!

JO

No, no, you don't.
We used to talk, we used to do things,
You used to tell me everything.
Now it's "John" this, and "John" that—

MEG

Jo—

JO

John, John, John—
That horrible ugly name!

MEG

But I do love you.
Of course I love you.
No sweeter sister, no dearer friend.
But once I saw him,
And once he looked at me...

(shrugs)
I can't explain it, Jo—
I love you—
Things end.
(Realizing that's too harsh, she backpedals.)
No—
Things change, Jo.
Things change.
You're a babe at the breast,
You're a daughter by the fire,
You have all the love you think you could desire.
Still,
Things change, Jo,
And, oh,
What happens when they do!
Your heart, Jo,
Your heart—
It's a bird in the nest
With its head beneath its wing:
Half asleep, it cannot know it wants a thing,
Still,
Your heart, Jo,
I know,
Will dream of something new:
Something that blurred, that broke within me,
A secret word—who was it?—spoke within me.
By some decree,
The girl I used to be—she's simply gone.
I cannot say, I do not know
Who stirred, who woke within me:
She loves her mother,
Loves her father,
Her sisters—
Of course,
(exalted)
But wants her John,
My John...
Things change, Jo—
Angels and pilgrims in heaven rejoice!

They change!
You're a rosebud in the night,
You're a blossom in the morn,
You're unmade by that light,
Yet reborn.
Things change—
And oh!
One day,
My Jo,
I wish only that things change
The same way
For you.
(*tenderly*)
Jo? Do you understand?

(*Jo stands immobile. From her viewpoint, Meg is abandoning her.*)

JO

I understand.
You're leaving us.
You're tearing a hole in the family.
I'll never forgive you as long as I live.

(*Meg freezes, then recovers.*)

MEG
(*shrugging*)

Well, I've tried, Jo.
One can only try.

(*She abandons Jo, vanishes into the dark. Jo slouches out of the hall, sinks wearily on the moonlit porch. From the dark, Laurie and Beth join her.*)

JO

Snow in October!
Who'd have thought?

BETH

I'm not much, I know;
But I'll stand by you, Jo, all the days of your life.

JO

Oh, Bethy...

(*Jo clasps Beth's hand. On her other side, Laurie squeezes her with deep feeling. Beth strokes her hair. Amy, nightgowned, materializes. She registers Laurie holding Jo. Now he's kissing her on top of her head. This is not the consolation Jo wants. Suddenly self-conscious, she pulls free of Laurie.*)

JO

I'm going upstairs.
Don't mind me.

(*She makes her way past Amy, who embraces her. Beth follows Jo. Amy and Laurie lock eyes.*)

AMY

Do you want to see a picture I drew?

LAURIE

My. It's the image of your father.
Has he seen it?

(*Jo has made her way upstairs, where pale light illuminates Meg's trunk.*)

AMY
(*crushed*)

It's supposed to be you.

(*Laurie shrugs. He gazes after Jo. Upstairs, Jo has collapsed in Beth's arms.*)

Scene Three

(*The March garden, the summer of the following year, Meg's wedding morning. Sunshine, flowers everywhere; the piano rolled outside. Alma, Gideon, a sullen Jo, Beth, Cecilia, and Amy, sketching.*)

AMY
(*displaying*)

Aunt?
Now, I haven't done any shading yet.

GIDEON

Already quarter past!

CECILIA
(to Amy)

Your line's improving.

ALMA

She was with him this morning.
He'd lost a button off his waistcoat.

CECILIA
(scandalized)

Meg was?
He's seeing her the wedding morning?

ALMA
(graciously)

Ours is not a superstitious home.

CECILIA

Alma, I so admire you.
Ever untroubled by questions of taste.
(to Amy)
We must speak about summer in Rome.

(Meg and Brooke rush in.)

MEG

Marmee.

GIDEON

At last!

BROOKE

We want to use your vows.

GIDEON

Our vows?

ALMA

You were going to write...

BROOKE

Nothing we came up with was nearly as beautiful.

ALMA

Wasn't Jo going to help you write your own?

MEG & BROOKE

Well...

BETH

She tried.

JO
(defensively)

I tried.

BETH & JO

"One can only try."

ALMA

Never mind. Beth?

(Beth crosses to Alma; then, at her behest, crosses to the piano.)

LAURIE
(entering, feverish and bright-eyed)

Jo?

JO
(arranging)

One moment.

AMY

Happy wedding, Laurie.

GIDEON
(to Meg)

You're sure?

MEG

Entirely.
Do you remember where you stored them?

ALMA

Other than in my heart?

CECILIA
(*embarrassed by Alma's effusiveness*)

I'm suffocating.

GIDEON

Cecilia.

CECILIA
(*defensively*)

It's the flowers.

BROOKE

Teach us.

JO

I'm ready.

LAURIE
(*to Jo*)

Wait.
(*He wants to hear the vows.*)

JO

Laurie, what is it?

ALMA

You know, children, Whitman was at our wedding.
(*She begins to sing the vows she and Gideon co-authored for their own wedding. Beth accompanies.*)

ALMA

We stand together on this old—

(*Beth suddenly faints at the keyboard. Jo rushes to her.*)

JO

Beth!

BETH

I'm fine. It's passed.

MEG

It's so warm out here, lamb—

BETH

I'm well, Meg, I am.

AMY

Beth!

BETH

I insist.
Mother, from the beginning?

ALMA

I won't resist you, dear.
We stand together on this new-old day,

GIDEON

Heart light, eyes seeing, eyes seeing ever—

ALMA

Firm on the willing earth, warm on the all-willing, welcoming earth.

ALMA & GIDEON

And I say shelter, ours the hours.
I say this moment, ours the hours.
I say hand joined to hand
To my beloved here I say,
I say ours the hours ever—
Ours the hours ever...
And...
But not without temper,
Not without trial,
Not without silence,
Not without tears.
But ever with ardor,
Ever with patience,
With the music of this covenant
Singing ever, singing ever in our ears.
So stand with us, beloved, on this everlasting day,
Robes white, voices raised, voices praising ever.
Sure of the eye of God, grateful, secure in the eye of God.

As we sing sacred, ours the hours,
We sing vocation, ours the hours,
We sing hand joined to hand.
To our beloved here we sing.
We sing ours the hours ever.
Ours the hours ever...
And...
Our lives a golden circle even as this ring.

                              LAURIE
                            (awed)
Jupiter Ammon! The poetry!

                              BROOKE
                       (a little appalled)
I thought you'd been raised Presbyterian.

                         ALMA & GIDEON
                           (proud)
Hardly.

                               MEG
Start them again, from the beginning.

                             CECILIA
Ah, the adorable quaintness of radicalism!

(Gideon is not amused.)

                              LAURIE
Let's go.

                               JO
Beth...

                              BETH
I'm fine. Go on.

                               JO
I love you.

                              BETH
I love you, too. Go on.

(Laurie and Jo withdraw to the hillock behind the March garden. Alma and Gideon are teaching Meg and Brooke their vows; their quartet, now accompanied by Beth at the piano, is still audible.)

MEG & BROOKE, ALMA & GIDEON

We stand together on this old-new day...

JO

What is it, Laurie?
Such a state!

LAURIE

You want to sit down?

JO

Ah—wait!
I understand now.

LAURIE

I have to clear my confounded throat.

MEG & BROOKE, ALMA & GIDEON

Eyes bright, hearts singing, hearts singing ever,
Under the singing sky…

JO

What a dunce I am!
I'm sorry, Laurie.
I should known by that look.

LAURIE

What?

MEG & BROOKE, ALMA & GIDEON

Under the high open world-winging sky…

JO

I'm all dismal at losing Meg,
But you, poor fellow—you're losing Brooke!

GIDEON

Again, from the beginning.

ALMA

Just for security.

LAURIE

No, Jo—

JO

I know—you fault yourself.
Don't, Laurie, you're not to blame.

LAURIE

Jo, let me speak!

MEG & BROOKE, ALMA & GIDEON

We stand together on this old-new day,
Eyes bright, hearts singing, hearts singing ever…

JO

And nothing else need change!
You and I and Beth and Amy,
All of us, forever just the same—

MEG & BROOKE, ALMA & GIDEON

Under the singing sky,
Under the high open world-winging sky…
And I say—

LAURIE
(abruptly)

Marry me! I love you.

JO

What on earth are you talking about?

LAURIE

I know you like me.
I've always liked you.
My *doppelgänger*, my partner in crime.
But I'm a man now,
And you're a woman, Jo—

JO
(*stubborn*)

No.

LAURIE

I don't know how I know,
But I do know
It's time,
It's time… things change, Jo, between us.
I've—

JO

Don't dare suggest it, Laurie:
We're perfect as we are!
Think how we enjoy each other,
Every day a game.
Married, we'd destroy each other—
We are far too much the same...

(*We see the rest of the family—all but Amy—performing the wedding.*)

MEG & BROOKE, ALMA & GIDEON

Not without temper,
Not without trial...

JO

We are far too much the same…

MEG & BROOKE, ALMA & GIDEON

Not without silence,
Not without tears...

LAURIE

My heart, Jo,
My heart!
It's beyond my control,
I am like a man possessed—
You cannot deny the one who loves you best,
Jo!

Jo

No, believe it, Laurie.
We're perfect as we are.
I'm far too fond of my own way,
And frankly, you are, too.
I could bring myself to say
"Love and honor"—
Not "obey"—
And neither, dear, could you!

MEG & BROOKE, ALMA & GIDEON

Singing ever, singing ever in our ears…

LAURIE

But something's blurred, something broke within me,
A secret word—who was it?—spoke within me.
By some decree,
The boy I used to be—where did he go?
I cannot say, I do not know
Who stirred, who woke within me—
He used to tease you,
Used to taunt you—
He liked you!
But now,
He loves his Jo,
My Jo…

Jo

I can't love you that way!

LAURIE

But might you change, Jo?
Might you change?
You could learn if you tried.
Would it be so hard a task?
Just you name it, I'll be anything you ask—
Please—

MEG & BROOKE, ALMA & GIDEON

So stand with us, beloved, on this everlasting day.
Robes white, voices raised, voices praising ever—

(Amy, unseen by Jo and Laurie, creeps in and eavesdrops.)

JO

(angry)

The staggering power your feelings wield!
You have to have me;
I have to yield.
What's to discuss?
"Your darling Laurie has changed,
Oh, yes, your Laurie has changed!
All you need do now is accept, Jo.
Adjust, Jo.
See, Laurie's changed,
So now, I fear,
You must, Jo."
I thought you'd understand.

MEG & BROOKE, ALMA & GIDEON

As we say promise, ours the hours.
We say tomorrow, ours the hours.
We say...

LAURIE

(cold)

I understand.
You don't love me.

JO

I do!

LAURIE

(agonized)

You're tearing a hole in my heart.
But I'll never forget you as long as I live.

JO

Laurie!

(He runs off. Amy appears from hiding.)

AMY

Your monstrous cruelty!
Crueler than ever I have seen!

JO

You don't know what you're talking about!

AMY

He loves you.
We, all of us, knew it.
You could see it in all he did and said.
And you treat him so coarsely,
And you treat him so coldly—

JO

You've got it so utterly wrong, Amy—

AMY

Kinder, really, just to shoot him dead!
Laurie!
(*She runs after him.*)

JO

Amy!

MEG & BROOKE, ALMA & GIDEON

Our lives a golden circle
Even as—

(*The piano—Beth's piano—suddenly jangles discordantly, as if someone had collapsed on the keys.*)

MEG

Beth!

ALMA

She can't stay out here, Gideon.

BROOKE

How can I help?

(*The family mills around Beth.*)

                                    Jo

Jo—let him go.
Just let him flee.
He'll be all right if you just let him be.
He'll just need a moment—
Or two—
(*Suddenly inspired*)
I know what I'll do. I know what I'll do!
(*She flees.*)

                                    MEG

Amy, Jo—
Somebody bring a cool cloth!

End of Act I

ACT II

Scene One

(The publishing offices of The Weekly Volcano, *a fiction tabloid based in New York City. One year later. Jo, terrified but feigning dignity, and Mr. Dashwood, perusing a manuscript. Dashwood raises an eyebrow.)*

DASHWOOD

"Cockling?"

JO

Cackling.

(Jo demonstrates. Dashwood holds up his hand. Jo falls mute. In her mind, Jo is acting out her beloved story, and, uncontrollably, starts to hum along with the orchestra. Dashwood observes her. Jo notices she's being noticed.)

DASHWOOD

Pray, proceed.

JO
(weakly)

"—And into the moat."
(apologetic)
I get excited.

DASHWOOD

She has a gift for the lurid manner.
This isn't your "friend's" first attempt, I take it?

JO

No, sir. She has some experience.
She's actually written for *The Blarneystone Banner.*

DASHWOOD

In Concord?

Jo

In Concord.

DASHWOOD

But now she's in New York.

Jo

That's so.

DASHWOOD

As of—when?

Jo

Year ago.

DASHWOOD

Runaway?

Jo

Indeed not.

DASHWOOD

Tragic romance?

Jo

Not if she can help it.

DASHWOOD

Tell me direct, Miss March—
This is a sensation sheet,
Not a home for wayward girls.

Jo

Her friend was getting too fond of her.
And her mother has a friend in New York.
So she thought she'd try out the city;
And give him some time to get
All of that nonsense out of his head.

DASHWOOD

Curious tactic.

Jo
(half to herself)

Things change, yes,
Things change—
But you give them some time,
And you try a different tack,
And I promise you that things change back!
What about my story?

DASHWOOD

Don't you mean *her* story?

Jo

My story.

DASHWOOD

Twenty-five dollars, payment when printed.
And you take out all the sermonizing.

Jo

Don't it need a moral?

DASHWOOD

We publish entertainment.
We don't need art.

Jo

I knew I liked you.
Thirty dollars, and two free copies.
I have sisters at home.

DASHWOOD

Done.

Jo

Done.

(They shake hands. Jo, triumphant, makes her way out.)

DASHWOOD

Poor, and proud as usual,
But she'll do.

(Now we are several places at once: Mrs. Kirke's boarding house in New York City; the March house; on tour in England. Jo and her family, in their respective locales, corresponding over some months. Jo has returned in triumph to her room in the New York boarding house of a friend of her mother's.)

Jo
(to Alma)

Drizzling in New York;
Still horridly loud,
And overcrowded;
But, more exciting,
I'm selling my writing
And making a fortune!
The stories I sell in New York
Are largely trash,
But oh! The cash!
Enclosed herein,
You'll find the beginnings of our fortune!
(delicately)
Give my love to everyone's favorite sophomore.

(Laurie appears in his Oxford room, studying. Jo looks his way. He ignores her.)

Jo
(hopefully)

Another month,
I know we'll be close as we were before.
(with bravado)
No, I haven't heard from him,
But I'm not concerned.
He wasn't exactly spurned.

(The family, reading Jo's letter, looks up, incredulous.)

Gideon & Alma

Not spurned?

Meg & Brooke

Not spurned?

AMY
(angry)

Ha!

JO
(guiltily)

Well, anyway,
Write soon.
Write soon.
Write soon, write soon, write soon,
Love—

(Friedrich Bhaer, bearded, impish, passes Jo on the way to his room. He waves. She waves.)

(Meg, who hasn't slept in weeks, appears in her kitchen, hollow-eyed but game.)

MEG
(to Jo)

Remember last month?
You know we were expecting,
But I was just a little late?
Prepare ye for a shock.

(Brooke, equally frayed from sleep deprivation, appears, shouldering twins. They wail, loudly.)

That's when there were two of us.
This month there are four of us,
And two of us expectorate
(a horribly telltale burp from one of the bundles on Brooke's shoulder)
Around the clock.

BROOKE
(reproachfully)

Daisy.

(Jo seems amused, but she hasn't forgiven Meg.)

MEG

Sister, don't mourn.
Truly, don't weep.
At least they're born,
And soon, I'm sure,
(a prayer)
I'll sleep—

(The babies wail again, more loudly then ever.)

MEG
(wailing)

John!

BROOKE
(roaring)

I'm trying!

MEG

Rock them,
Sing to them, anything!

BROOKE

Laudanum!
(Insanely inspired, he dashes off to ransack the kitchen for tincture of opium.)

MEG

Write soon, *please,*
Write soon.
Write soon, write soon, write soon—
Laudanum?
(She dashes off to save her husband from himself.)

(Amy appears, grandly dressed, in her London hotel room.)

AMY
(editing)

Dear L—
Darling Lawrence—
Mr. Theodore—
(She gives up.)

Laurie, I'm in England: Aunt has subsidized my tour.
I've plenty to amuse me, and you're studying, I'm sure.
But I'm here at least a fortnight, so if ever you are free,
We could always meet for tea.

(Laurie, from his dormitory room, looks her way.)

AMY

Write soon.
Write soon.
Write soon, write soon, write soon—
Fondly...
(She likes that "fondly.")

(Alma appears, tending a bedridden Beth.)

ALMA
(forcing cheer)

Beth loves the music,
Thinks you're a dear!
She'd love to go to the seaside, Jo—

ALMA & BETH

But not this year—

BETH

Just too much moving—

ALMA

—Is all she'll say.
Is she improving?
Well,
(frankly)
It's day by day.
(pleading)
Write soon.
Write soon.
Write soon, write soon,
Love—

JO

Professor Bhaer, Father,
German teacher, tiny room across from mine?
(*Bhaer appears at her door, cloaked, with opera tickets.*)
(It's a cave!)
Just light supper, then the opera.

GIDEON
(*concerned*)

How old is he?

JO

Not to worry—
Thirty-nine!
(*laughing*)
One foot in the grave!
(*She shoulders into her evening cloak.*)

AMY, BETH, MEG, JO, ALMA, LAURIE, BROOKE, GIDEON

Write soon,
Write soon,
Write soon, write soon, write soon,
Love…

(*Jo and Bhaer are off.*)

Scene Two

(*Again, different locations simultaneously: Jo's corridor in the boarding house, late that night after the opera; and Oxford, a sunny weekday afternoon. Jo and Bhaer arrive onstage, in evening dress, returning from some overripe melodrama. But they've clearly had a terrific time. Gradually they make their way to Jo's door.*)

JO

But that's why I loved it! So lurid and preposterous.
Though I would have liked to understand the words.

BHAER
(*grandly*)

Italians make opera.
They do not make art.

JO

You'd love my father, Professor.

BHAER

Please—
Friedrich.

JO

Friedrich.
Couldn't they just print the words on a banner,
Unspool it in front of the stage,
So you could read what they were saying as they sing it—

BHAER

It never would work, Miss March.

JO

Please—
Jo.

BHAER

Jo?

JO

What?

BHAER

Isn't Jo a boy's name?

JO

My father is a man.
I take after his side of the family.

(*In a sunny lane on Oxford's campus, Amy appears, sketching a lounging Laurie.*)

LAURIE

Your father is a man.
Does she take after his side of the family?

AMY
(laughing)

But that was always Jo!
Elbows out, nose in the air,
Calling it independence.
Hold still.

LAURIE

I liked that about her.

AMY
(delicately)

But she was right, you know.
You quarreled like magpies.

LAURIE

They always blew over.

AMY

So Roman a profile...

LAURIE

Amy, you were touring in Rome.
What brought you to England?

(Amy looks at Laurie. Jo and Bhaer reappear.)

JO

What brought you to America?

AMY & BHAER

Interest.

(For a moment we see and hear, in slanting afternoon light, a pale and driven Beth, at her piano, trying to compose a satisfactory ending to her chorale.)

BHAER

Interest. So lively a country!
And there was nothing waiting for me in Berlin.

JO

Meaning?

BHAER

And no one for me either.
(*parrying*)
You're a little young to be on your own in New York.

Jo

The matron's a school friend of my mother's.
She looks after me.

BHAER

What brought you here?

Jo

Strategy.

BHAER

Meaning?

Jo

A friend decided he was in love with me.
And I despise that nonsense.

BHAER

Is it such nonsense?

Jo

Yes.

Jo & Laurie

We were such devoted friends!

Amy

And yet you squabbled all the time.

Laurie

Well, she was strong-minded.

Amy

Strong of mind, Laurie?
Or merely strong of will?
Your hair is blowing. How long it's gotten!

LAURIE

Is marriage so awful?

AMY & JO

I think marriage is the—

AMY

Best—

JO

Worst—

AMY & JO

Possible thing for a woman.

BHAER

So do I.

JO
(delighted)

You do?

BHAER
(shrugging)

Too many men bind a woman into marriage
Like a groom strapping a horse into harness.
And too many women call that love.
Seems to me you both pull together,
Or no one pulls at all.

JO
(amazed)

That's just what I told my sister Meg!
Not in so many words.

BHAER

Which were your words?

JO

Well...

(Jo and Laurie whinny. Bhaer looks confused. Amy laughs.)

JO & LAURIE

It's a long story.

AMY
(laughing)

Poor Meg! Poor Brooke!
How long ago it all seems.

LAURIE

Things change, Amy.

AMY

And a good thing, too!
(displaying)
There.
Now, I haven't done any shading yet.

LAURIE

How well you draw!

AMY & JO

It helps to have a subject.

(Midnight. Beth at her piano, paler and more driven than before. She plays her chorale; she still cannot end it. Suddenly—as if the piece stands for everything that defeats her— she flings herself at the keyboard, pounding the same chord over and over. Alma, nightgowned, appears, puzzled and frightened. Beth stares at her. They understand each other.)

JO

It helps to have a subject.
But it's better to have a style.

BHAER

Ah, yes. Your sensation stories.

JO

You disapprove.

BHAER

I didn't say that.

Jo

They're keeping my family in comforts.

Bhaer

Comforts are comforting.

Jo
(circling him)

"The Bloodstained Hand" laid a new carpet.

Bhaer

Applaud that hand!

Jo
(strutting)

"The Daughter of the Coventries"
Sent my sister to the seaside.
(cavilling)
Not that she'd go.

Bhaer

Conscientious daughter!

Jo

And "Behind a Mask"...

Bhaer

...Is who?

Jo
(defensively)

Just me.
(mocking)
Not a genius like Keats.
(challenging)
My father's been writing for twenty years, and
He's never earned like I do.
There's a market for this.

Bhaer

There's a market for opium, too.
You can do better than this, Jo.

AMY

Certain to rain any moment—

AMY & BHAER

I sense it.

LAURIE

I'll walk you to your carriage?

AMY

I would like that.

AMY & LAURIE

Good day.
Good day.
(*Amy and Laurie vanish.*)

JO
(*unsure*)

I *would* like that—
To do something truly grand before I die.
But not tonight.
Besides, what's your alternative?

BHAER

What are you asking?

JO

Well, if the opera isn't,
And my stories aren't,
What's "proper" art?

BHAER

Is that a serious question?

JO

Serious as I get.

BHAER

See how this compares to *The Blarneystone Banner*.
(*reciting*)
Kennst du das land wo die Zitronen blühn?
Im dunkeln Laub die Gold-Orangen glühn,

Ein sanfter Wind vom blauen Himmel weht,
Die Myrte still, und hoch der Lorbeer steht.
Kennst du es wohl?
Dahin! Dahin!
O mein Geliebter, möcht ich mit dir,
O mein Geliebter, ziehn.

                              JO

Your voice is beautiful.
Though I still would like—

                          JO & BHAER

—To understand the words.

(Bhaer laughs.)

                            BHAER

"Do you know the land where the lemon trees bloom,
And oranges like gold amid the leafy gloom?
A gentle wind from bluest heaven blows,
The myrtle green, and high the laurel grows.
Do you know that land?
'Tis there! Ah! 'Tis there!
O my beloved,
Ah—'tis there I dream we would go."
Goethe. *Wilhelm Meisters Lehrjahre.*

                              JO

It's lovely.
My father swears by him.
(provoking him into confrontation, to break the mood)
What if I love Goethe *and* the opera?

                            BHAER

I would laud you as a strong-minded woman.

                              JO

Oh! Good.
This is the most fun I've had since I left home.

(They're at her door. To it is tacked a telegram. Jo tears it open.)

BHAER

Is everything well?

JO
(reading)

No. No, it can't be.

(Cold light finds Alma.)

ALMA
(barely controlled)

Come as soon as you can—stop.
Beth. The fever—stop.

JO
(dazed)

I have to go home.

BHAER

I can take you.

JO
(near panicked)

No!

ALMA

Your loving mother—stop.

JO

Forgive me.
It's my sister.
I have to go.

BHAER

Let me drive you to the station.

JO

Friedrich!
This is my family.
I have to go.

BHAER

I'll write you.

(Jo flees. We still see Alma.)

ALMA

Come as soon as you can—stop.
Beth. The fever—stop.
Your loving mother—stop.
(losing control)
Beth. The fever—stop.
Beth. The fever—stop.
Beth. The fever—stop.
Stop!

Scene Three

(Beth's bedroom, three sleepless days later. Beth, translucent, dozing on a throne of pillows, ringed by Gideon, Alma, Meg and Brooke. Cecilia is there too, watchful from a far corner. A disheveled Jo rushes in, crushes her face into Alma's shoulder.)

GIDEON

She's asked for you.

(Jo rushes to the bed and kneels.)

BETH
(faintly)

Is that my Jo?

JO

Here, oh, here, dear!

BETH

Everyone, leave us a moment?
Thank you.

(For an invalid, Beth wields a lot of authority. The family withdraws.)

BETH

Remember?

Nearly two years now: Truth or Fabrication?
Eight years short, I fear.

Jo

Don't be morbid, angel.
I'm here now, and I won't leave you
Till you're well and rosy again.

(Beth looks at her.)

BETH

Jo against the world!

Jo
(chatty)

You've heard from Amy, I expect?
Spring, she's coming home.

BETH
(wanting none of this)

My warrior.
My Jo!

Jo

She never writes me anymore.
I can't imagine why.
I've written her reams.

BETH

With your hot furrowed brow,
With your mad, flashing eye,
Who could ever dare deny you, dear?
Not I!

Jo

And Laurie—
Regardless.
Anyway, there you'll be.
Running down the path to greet her...

BETH

Still—

JO
(frenzied)

No one dies of scarlet fever anymore.

BETH

Well—

JO

The Hummels survived scarlet fever.

BETH

Actually—

JO

Two of them did!
Why is there no air in here?

BETH
(pleading)

My angel—

JO

You're suffocating!

BETH

Let go!

JO

Concord doctors!

BETH

We're together for now.

JO

No wonder you're poorly.

BETH

We'll be happy while we wait.
Don't let's waste a moment arguing with fate—

Jo

These towels!

BETH

Please—

Jo
(deaf to her)

I know.
The seaside, Beth:
I've got the money saved.
It won't take us that long to pack.

BETH
(wearily)

Oh, Jo.

Jo
(with mad gaiety)

A simple change of atmosphere,
A simple change of atmosphere,
A different atmosphere.

BETH

Jo! Jo! Jo! Jo—Jo—
Shh.
(She draws Jo to her.)
Have peace, Jo.
It's best, Jo.
Release, soon,
Then rest.
We'll not weep.
We'll not fight.
Just sleep, soon,
And then only light.
Only light.
Be reconciled,
Reconciled to my lot.
You are tomorrow's child.
I am not.

Of course, I—
I never had a future planned—
We'd thought that odd,
Remember?
Now we understand—

Jo
(breaking free)

No!

BETH
(serenely)

We understand!

Jo

Beth!

BETH
(ecstatic)

It was the hand of God,
Gentle and true,
Guiding me to the blessed, blessed meadow...

Jo

You promised you'd be with me all the days of my life.
I need more days than this.

BETH
(gentle, implacable)

Things change, Jo.
Cherish and promise and dream as we may;
They change.
Tell the tide not to turn,
Tell the sun not to rise,
Try, forbid the snow from falling from the skies?
No.
(She grasps Jo's hand.)
Mother and Father—you're all they've got now.
Promise me you'll take care of them.

JO

I promise.

BETH
(relieved)

I love you, Jo, so much.
How poorly I slept last night!
Just let me close my eyes a minute.

(She dozes. Jo stands vigil.)

QUARTET OF FEMALE VOICES

She who is down need fear no fall,
She who is low, no pride,
She who is humble ever shall
Have God to be her guide.
I am content with what I have,
Naught be it or much...

(The voices trail off. Jo, startled from sleep, looks down at Beth.)

JO

Beth. Beth!

(The family returns. Alma and Gideon make their farewells to their daughter and draw the coverlet over her. Jo, distraught, turns to her former confidant...)

JO

Meg?

(...but Meg has buried her face in her husband's shoulder.)

JO
(in wonder)

I've lost you all.

(In the attic, Beth's trunk glows in a shaft of light.)

Scene Four

(The path in front of the March house, the following spring. Jo, a wraith in a dark dress, sweeping the front steps. Cecilia, nearby, playing solitaire.)

CECILIA

That's the trouble with solitaire:
You always need a king.
(Jo sweeps.)
Grim homecoming, really.
Marital bliss notwithstanding.

JO

Marmee wired them not to come then.
It would have taken a month on the ship.
And Beth would have wanted their happiness.

CECILIA
(baiting)

Have you read Amy's letter?

JO

Your tone tells me you have.

(Cecilia hands it to her.)

JO

My.
"Joy beyond measure, Mother!"

(Amy appears, radiant beyond imagining. Laurie is visible behind her. He and Jo lock eyes.)

AMY

Joy beyond measure, Mother!
Happier than ever I have been!
It's happened.
At last, it's happened.
I feel it in all he say and does.
And it makes me so happy,
And it makes me so humble

That I'm not at all the same girl I was.
For I am loved.
I am loved.
Loved beyond compare…

AMY & LAURIE

Loved, loved beyond belief.
As we say promise, ours the hours.
We say forever, ours the hours.
We say hand joined to hand.
To our beloved here we say; we say
Ours the hours ever,
Ours the hours ever,
And...
(Laurie disappears.)

AMY

We'll come home in the Spring.
Love to everyone.
If only Bethy could have seen us.
(She fades from view.)

JO

She sounds very happy.
I hope Laurie feels the same.

CECILIA

And you feel?

JO

Very old.

CECILIA
(gentler)
That German teacher—has he written?

JO

I'm sure he's got better things to do.

(Cecilia watches her a moment.)

CECILIA

I'm proud of you, Josephine.
You're learning wisdom.

JO
(laughing weakly)

I haven't learned anything.

CECILIA

Indeed you have.
Last year your sister, this teacher
Would have broken your heart.
This year, you hardly notice them.
(Jo shrugs.)
There's something you should know.
I'm leaving you Plumfield.

JO

You are?

CECILIA

I've revised my will.
The house, the library, the orchard—
All yours.

JO
(stunned)

Thank you, Aunt. But—

CECILIA

Why?
Because now you can appreciate them.
Consider:
You, alone,
A mansion of stone,
Gated with steel.
Might it appeal?
The books, the art,
An empire apart.
Serene, secure,
You see the allure.
Lovers lie.

Others leave,
Over and over
And over and over again.
Cry.
Grieve.
But, then—
What then?

                              Jo
                        (*admitting*)
People change. You cannot change them.
Things stay as you arrange them.

                              CECILIA
Precisely.

                              Jo
I, alone—

                              CECILIA
You, alone—

                              Jo
A mansion of stone.

                              CECILIA
Alone in a mansion of stone.

                              Jo
Completely defended.

                              CECILIA
Believe me, it's splendid.

                              Jo
The pearls—

                              CECILIA
My mother's pearls—

                              Jo
The satin—

CECILIA

The laces, the garnets...

JO

Ovid—in English?

CECILIA
(*scornfully*)

My dear!
Mine is a civilized household.

JO

Completely protected.

CECILIA

There's naught unexpected.
Lovers...

JO

Sisters, friends lie.

CECILIA

Passions alter.
Others...

JO

Each of them, all of them leave.

CECILIA

Friendships falter
Over and over…

CECILIA & JO

And over and over again.

CECILIA

Hear me, Jo.
Cry—

JO

Cry, cry, cry—

CECILIA

Love controls you.

CECILIA

Grieve, grieve...

JO

Grieve, grieve.

CECILIA

Wealth, wealth consoles you.

JO

But, then...

CECILIA

Learn what I know.

JO

What then?

CECILIA

What then?

CECILIA & JO

People change. You cannot change them.
Things stay as you arrange them.

CECILIA

Perfect as they are.
Ever perfect as they are.

JO
(a scream)

Wait!

CECILIA

Josephine?

(Jo thinks about it a moment.)

JO

I alone,
A mansion of stone,
Bejeweled, becalmed.

(Cecilia's delighted she's getting it.)

                                        CECILIA

Dependent on no one, nothing—

(Jo looks directly at Cecilia as she continues.)

                                        JO

Well-dressed, well-read,
Essentially dead,
Though not yet embalmed—

                                        CECILIA
                                        (stunned)

Josephine!

                                        JO

Aunt, forgive me—
I know you mean well.
But that—that isn't living—
It's more a living h...

                                        CECILIA
                                        (livid)

This entire family is insane.
Was Gideon adopted?

                                        JO

I'm sorry.
(She flees indoors.)

                                        CECILIA
                                        (furiously)

Cry, cry,
Grieve, grieve.
But, then—
What then?
(softly)
What now?

Scene Five

(The same attic we saw at the beginning, with the four chests. Jo storms in.)

Jo
(frantic)

So the days go by,
And the summers fly,
And the lovers and the angels
Crowd around my sisters' doors.
And things change, Jo.
Oh, yes, things change, Jo.
What endures?
What endures?
(She flings herself at her notebook, scribbles madly for a moment—then flings it away. She retrieves the notebook. She waits. She begins again.)

QUARTET OF FEMALE VOICES

Four little chests all in a row,
Dim with dust and worn by time,
All fashioned and filled long ago
By children now in their prime.

(Laurie—vital, handsome, nervous today—has opened the attic door, and the lampglow from downstairs shines in. It's the beginning all over again.)

Jo

Laurie!

LAURIE

The very same, Madam.

Jo

Christopher Columbus! Look at you.

LAURIE

I've hardly changed.

Jo

Small ways.
Bigger. Bonnier. Otherwise,
The same scapegrace as always.

LAURIE

It's wonderful to see you, Jo…

JO & LAURIE

So…

LAURIE

Jo,
Can you forgive me?

JO

Laurie.
Forgive you?
(*laughing*)
Just tell me one thing.

LAURIE

Ask it.

JO

Who obeys?
Amy or my boy?

LAURIE

Now you're beginning to marm it!
I'd hoped I could count on you—
I should have known I could!
Ah, Jo!
So we can be just best friends again,
Best friends for good.
You know, Jo, it was truly perfect—perfect—
Perfect as it was.
Perfect as it wa—

JO

What did you say?

LAURIE

Wasn't it perfect as it was?

JO

No.
(speaking)
I'm happy for you, Laurie, with all my heart; but the old times can't come back, and we mustn't expect it. We are man and woman now, with sober work to do. I'm sure you see the change in me, and I in you. I shall miss my boy, but I shall love the man as much, for he means to be what I hoped he would, and we can be brother and sister, to love and help each other all our lives, won't we, Laurie?

LAURIE
(tenderly)

I'm glad to hear you say it.

JO

My Laurie.
Go, tell them all I'll be down in a moment.

(Laurie returns downstairs. Jo opens the chests, ruefully dons her moustache.)

JO

Barristers! It's quarter past!

(And from nowhere, phantasms of Meg, Beth, and Amy materialize; not the three young women we saw last, but the girls they were, years ago.)

MEG, BETH, AMY

Again we meet to celebrate
With badge and solemn rite,
Our fifty-second anniversary—

AMY

Fifty-first—Meg's cold—

JO

No.
(She takes off her moustache. The sisters pause.)
No games now.
No fairy stories, no "let's pretend."
I'd asked for a moment:
This is the moment.
I understand now.
You love me—

Things end.
Still—
(*with infinite tenderness*)
Let me look at you—
Golden—
The angels I recall.
A sisterhood of summer,
What did we know of fall?
What could we know of fall?
Who will we be tomorrow?
It's not in my control.
I know, though, for a moment,
We were four sisters,
One soul.

(*The sisters approach Jo.*)

MEG

I, too, remember us.

BETH

Golden.

AMY

Happy and at play.

BETH & MEG

Our perfect summer came to pass;
It didn't come to stay.

AMY, BETH, MEG

It couldn't come to stay.
Where'er we are tomorrow,
How near, how far apart,
Still, for a moment,
We were four sisters,
One heart.

JO

Who was that frightened child
Trying to postpone
What had to be,

Clinging, clinging to what was?
Unenlightened child!
Shouldn't she have known
What had to be?
Well, now she does—
Now she does.
(She walks to Meg's chest.)
Meg—you've found your knight.
I wish the world to him, and to his wife.
(Jo closes the chest.)
Bethy—you were right.
You will stand by me every moment of my life.
(She closes Beth's chest.)
Amy—we cease our fighting.
At last you have your Laurie for your own!
(She closes Amy's chest.)
And me, well, I'm still writing,
And still alone.
Still alone.
(She closes her own chest.)

Jo

Still, I'll remember us,

BETH

Chatting,

MEG

Pouting,

AMY

Spatting,

Jo

Shouting,

AMY, BETH, MEG, JO

Still—
How happy we were then!
A half-enchanted family
We'll never be again.

We will never be that way again.
Enough! On to tomorrow,
Each to her separate goal.
Still, for a moment—
Remember the moment!
We were four sisters,
(They pause, hands joined, to embroider on this vocally.)
One soul.
One soul.
One soul.

(Embracing Jo in turn, the sisters begin to fade away.)

Jo

How grateful I am...

(And Jo is alone. But someone has opened the attic door, again, and the lampglow from downstairs shines in.)

Jo

Laurie?

(A head becomes visible in the opening; bearded, bright-eyed, nervous today.)

Jo

Friedrich!

BHAER

I had a little business in town.
Is now the good moment?

(She thinks a moment.)

Jo

Now is all there is.
(She extends her hand.)
Come in.

(He ascends towards her.)

End of opera